Color by Sight Word

Sparkling Minds

SIGHT WORDS

Pre-K

a	funny	look	see
and	go	make	the
away	help	me	three
big	here	my	to
blue	I	not	two
can	in	one	up
come	is	play	we
down	it	red	where
find	jump	run	yellow
for	little	said	you

kindergarten

all	four	out	this
am	get	please	too
are	good	pretty	under
at	have	ran	want
ate	he	ride	was
be	into	saw	well
black	like	say	went
brown	must	she	what
but	new	so	white
came	no	soon	who
did	now	that	will
do	on	there	with
eat	our	they	yes

First Grade

after	give	let	some
again	going	live	stop
an	had	may	take
any	has	of	thank
as	her	old	them
ask	him	once	then
by	his	open	think
could	how	over	walk
every	just	put	were
fly	know	round	when
from			

Second Grade

always	don't	or	upon
around	fast	pull	us
because	first	read	use
been	five	right	very
before	found	sing	wash
best	gave	sit	which
both	goes	sleep	why
buy	green	tell	wish
call	its	their	work
cold	made	these	would
does	many	those	write
	off		your

a - pink   look - blue   and - black   make - green
funny - brown   see - orange   go - red   the - yellow

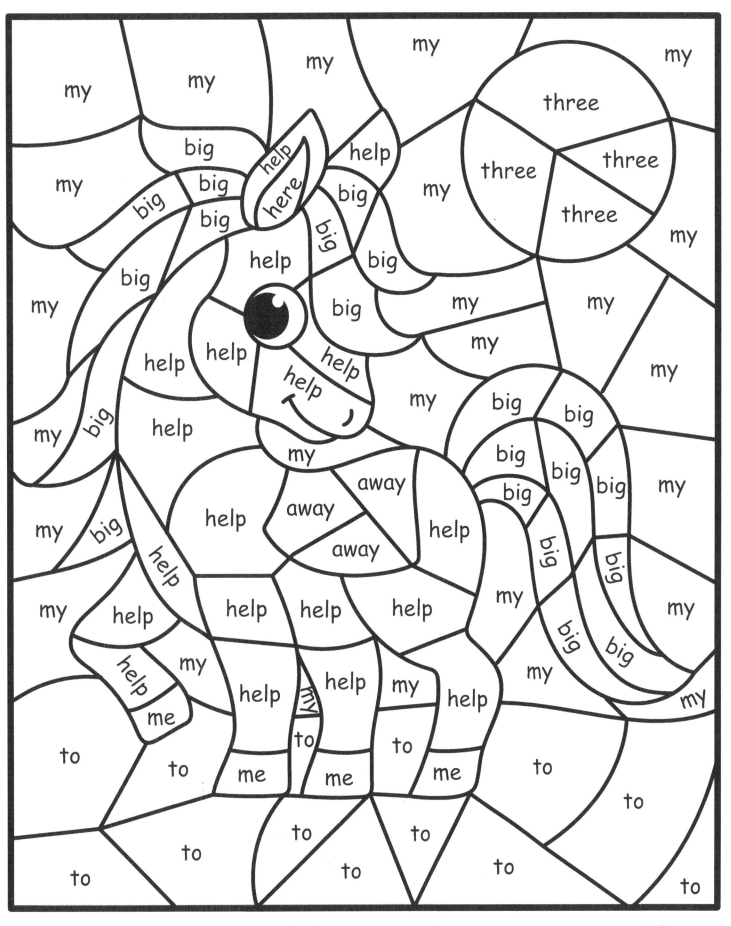

away - red   me - black   big - orange   my - blue

help - brown   three - yellow   here - pink   to - green

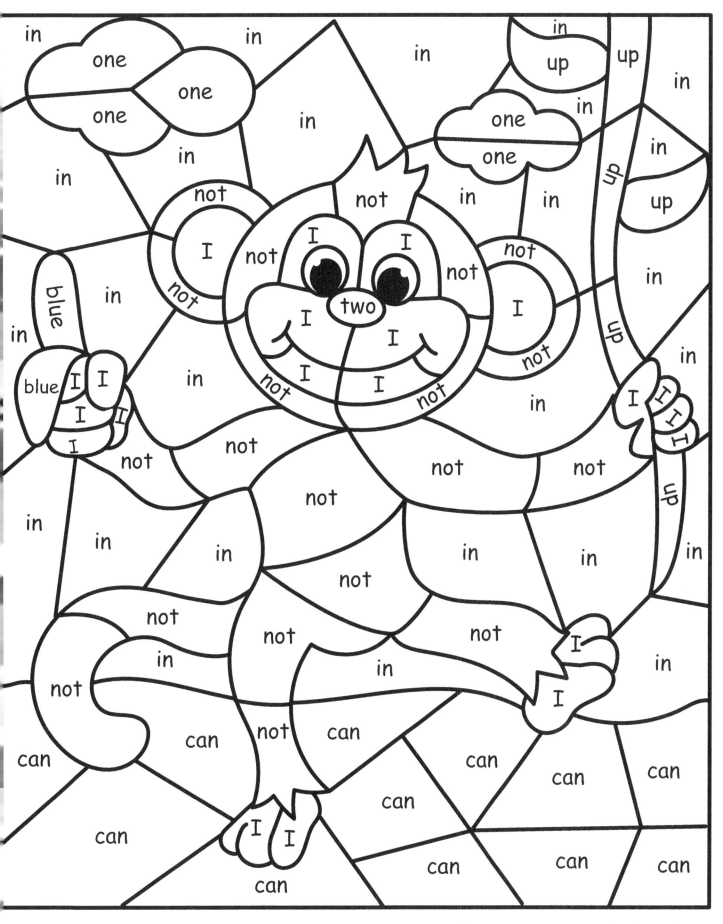

blue - yellow   not - dark brown   can -dark green   one - light blue

I - light brown   two - black   in - dark blue   up - light green

come - black   it - red   down - dark green   red - light green

where - blue   we - yellow   play - dark brown   is - light brown

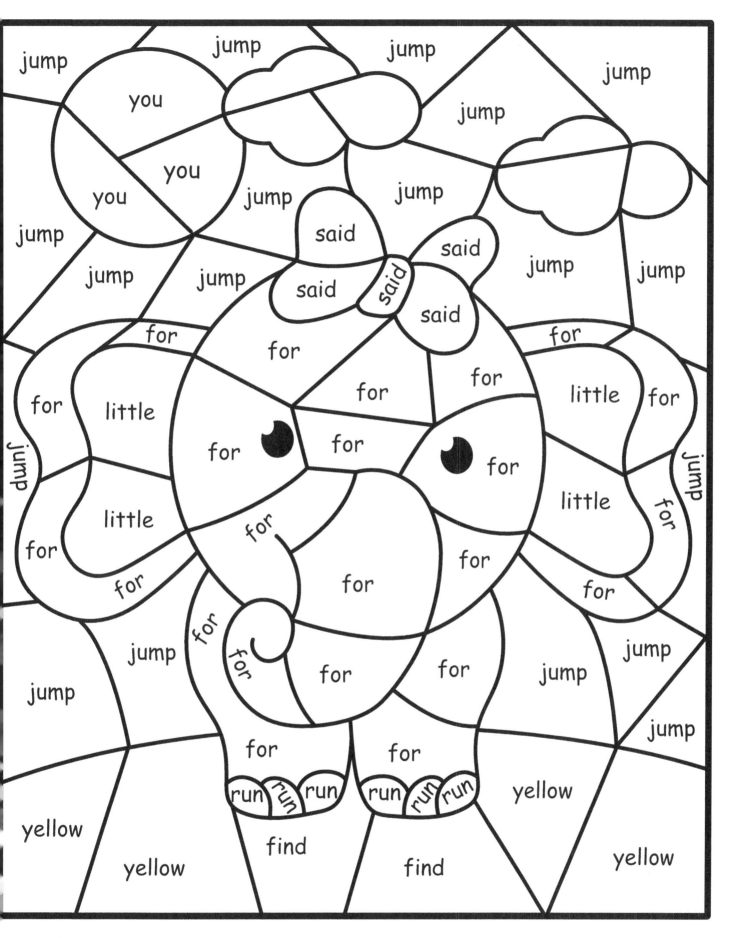

find - dark brown   run - light brown   for - gray   said - red

jump - blue   yellow - green   little - pink   you - yellow

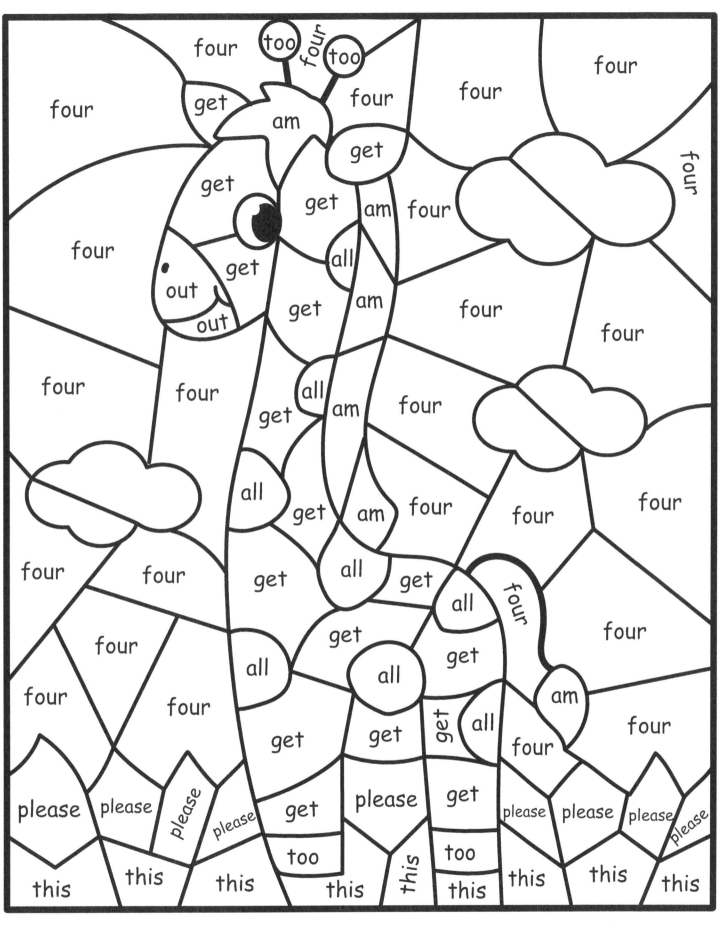

all - orange   too - black   am - brown   please - light green

get - yellow   this - dark green   four - blue   out - light pink

under - dark green   good - yellow   have - orange   ran - black

are - pink   at - brown   pretty - blue   want - light green

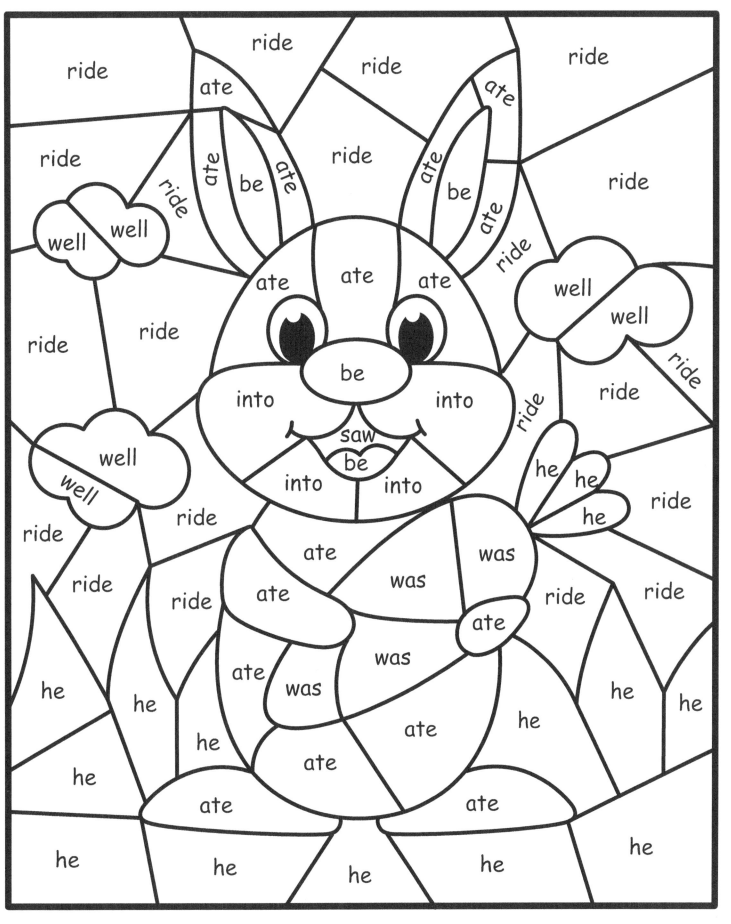

ate - gray   ride - dark blue   be - pink   saw - black

he - green   was - orange   into - yellow   well - light blue

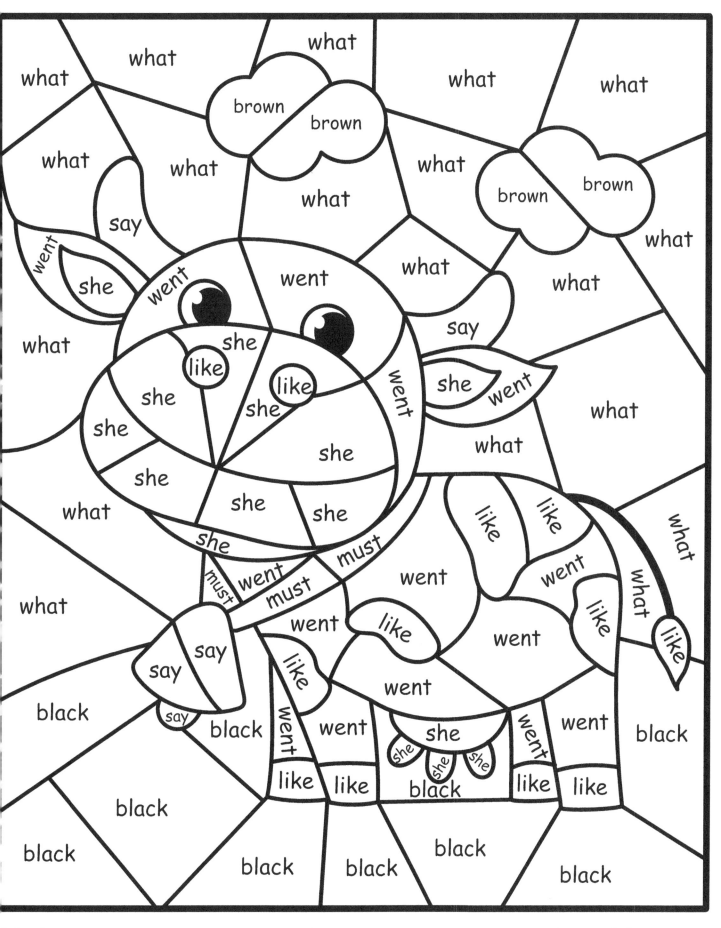

black - green
like - black
brown - light blue
went - light brown
must - red
say - yellow
she - pink
what - dark blue

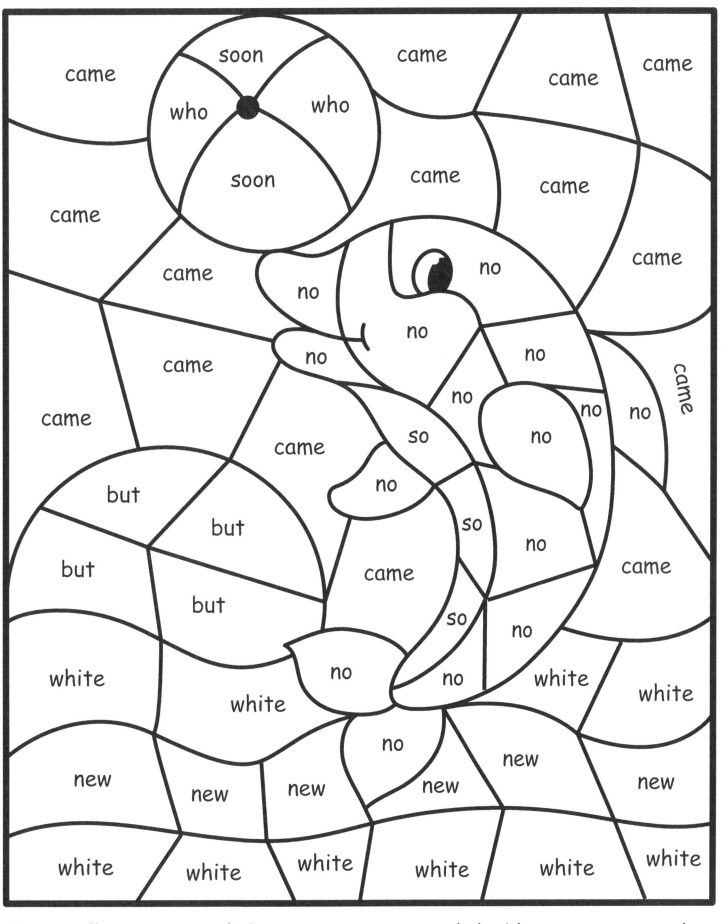

but - yellow   so - light gray   came - light blue   soon - red

new - dark blue   white - light green   no - dark gray   who - pink

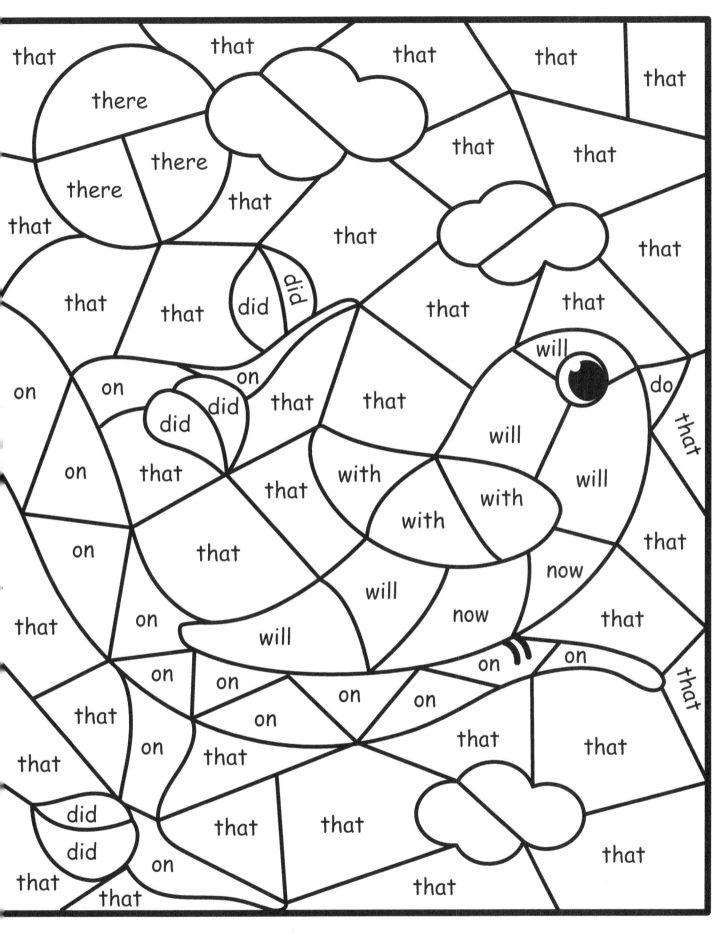

did - green   that - blue   do - orange   there - yellow

now - light purple   will - dark purple   on - brown   with - pink

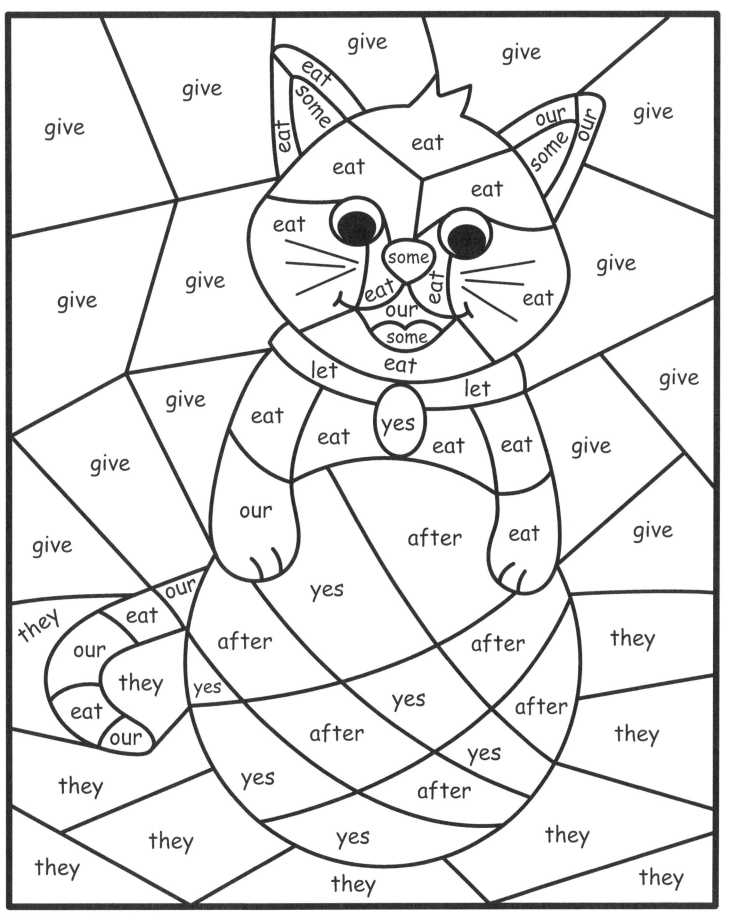

eat - light brown   they - dark purple   some - pink   give - light purple

our - black   yes - yellow   let - red   after - dark blue

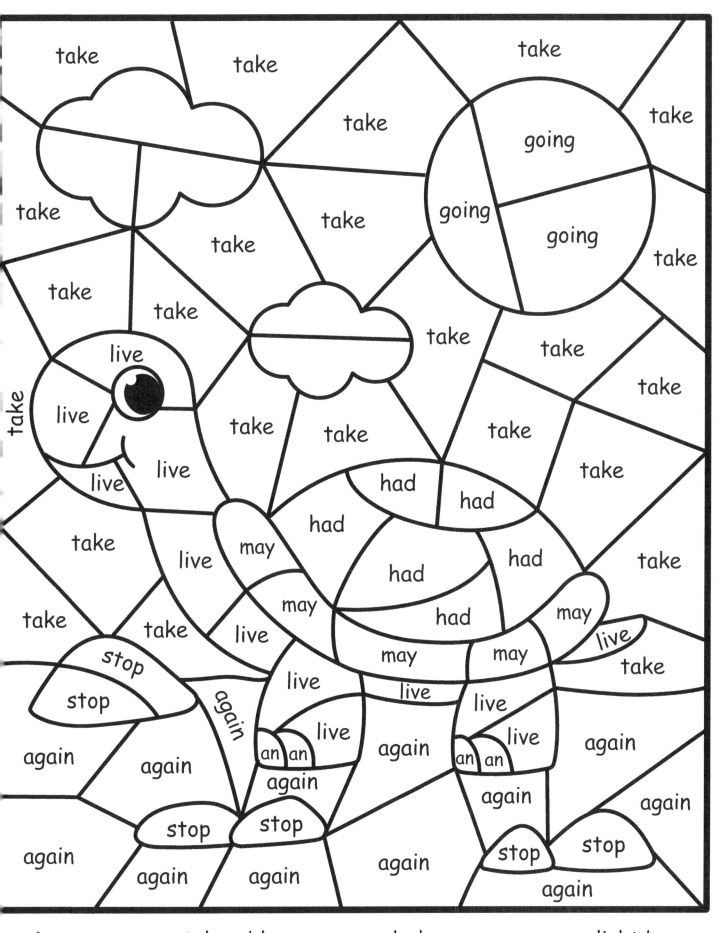

again - orange   take - blue   an - dark green   may - light brown

going - yellow   stop - gray   had - dark brown   live - light green

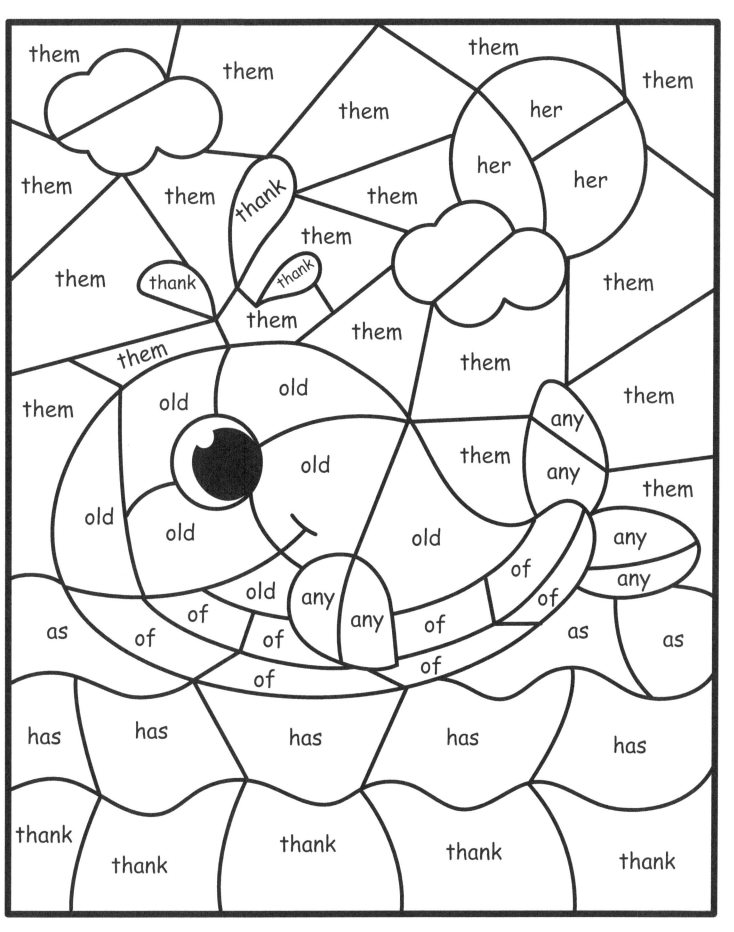

as - light green   of - light purple   has - dark green   old - dark purple
any - dark pink   thank - dark blue   her - yellow   them - light blue

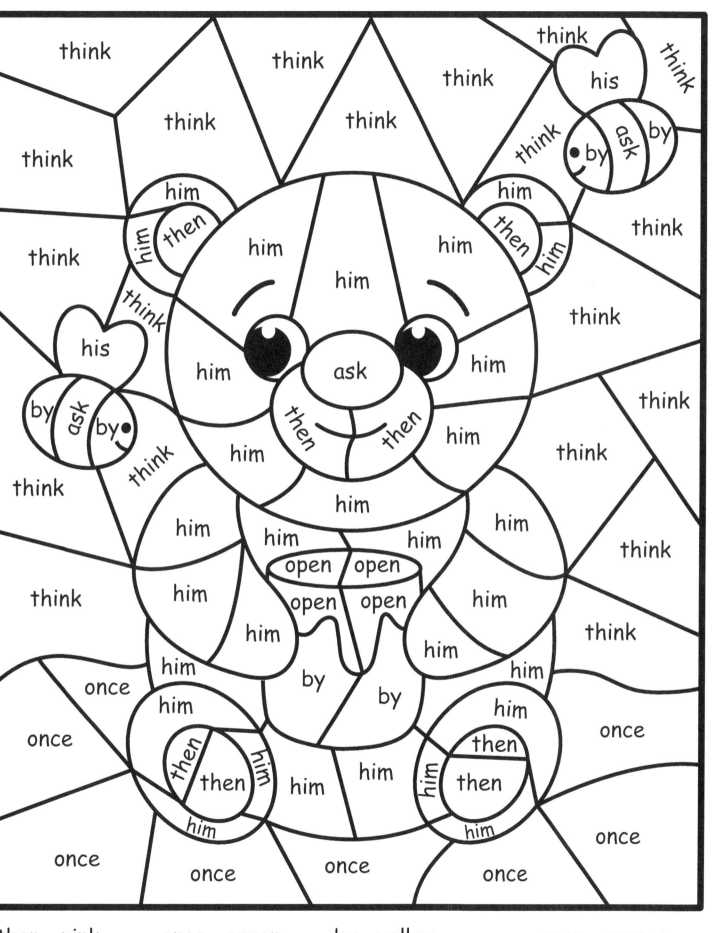

then - pink   once - green   by - yellow   open - orange
him - brown   ask - black   his - light blue   think - dark blue

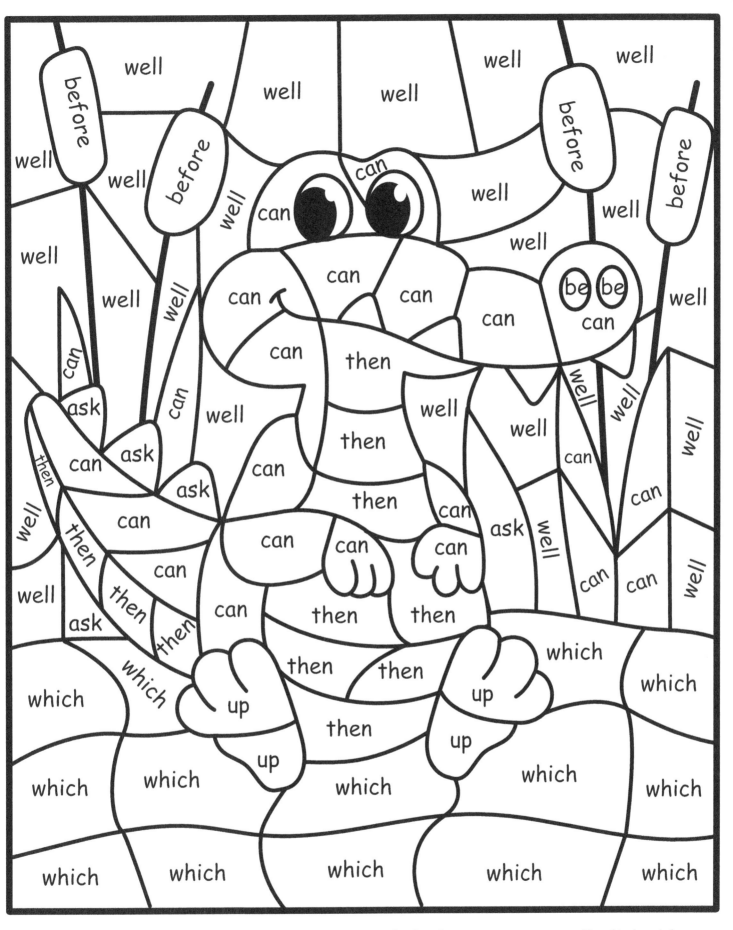

then - yellow   ask - dark green   up - light brown   well - light blue

be - black   can - light green   before - dark brown   which - dark blue

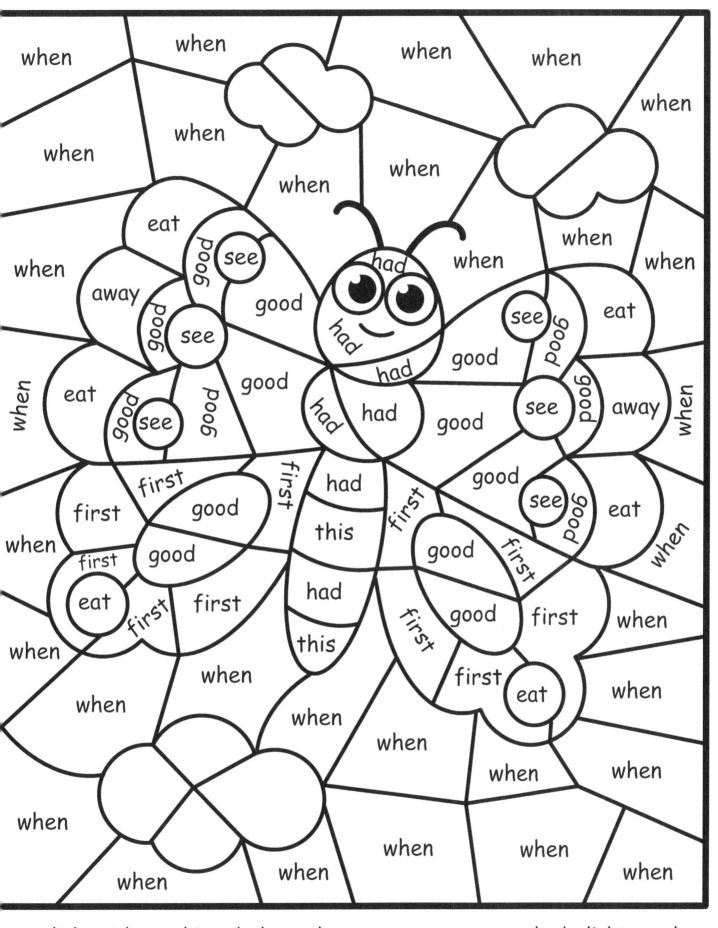

see - light pink   this - dark purple   away - orange   had - light purple

eat - red   when - dark blue   good - dark pink   first - yellow

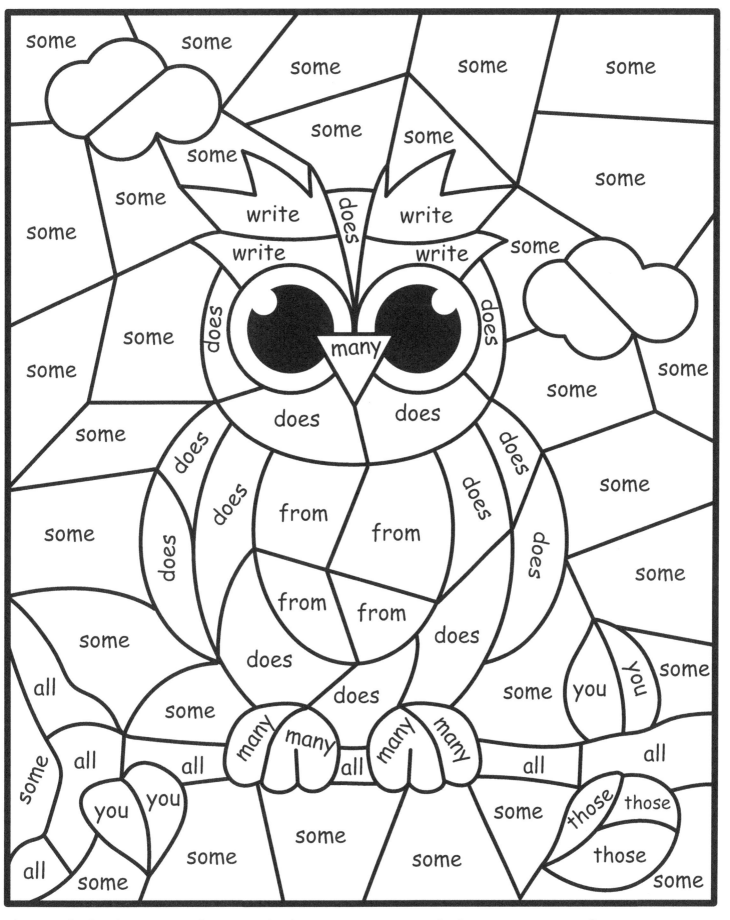

does - light brown   those - dark green   you - light green   from - orange

many - yellow   write - red   all - dark brown   some - blue

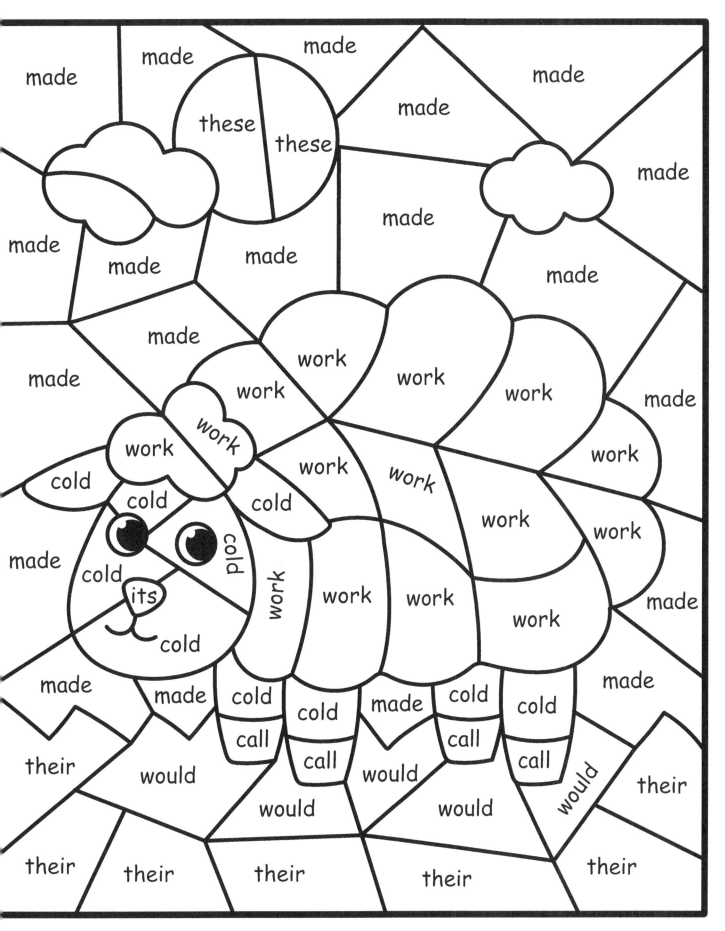

call - black   their - dark green   cold - light pink   these - yellow

its - dark pink   work - light brown   made - blue   would - light green

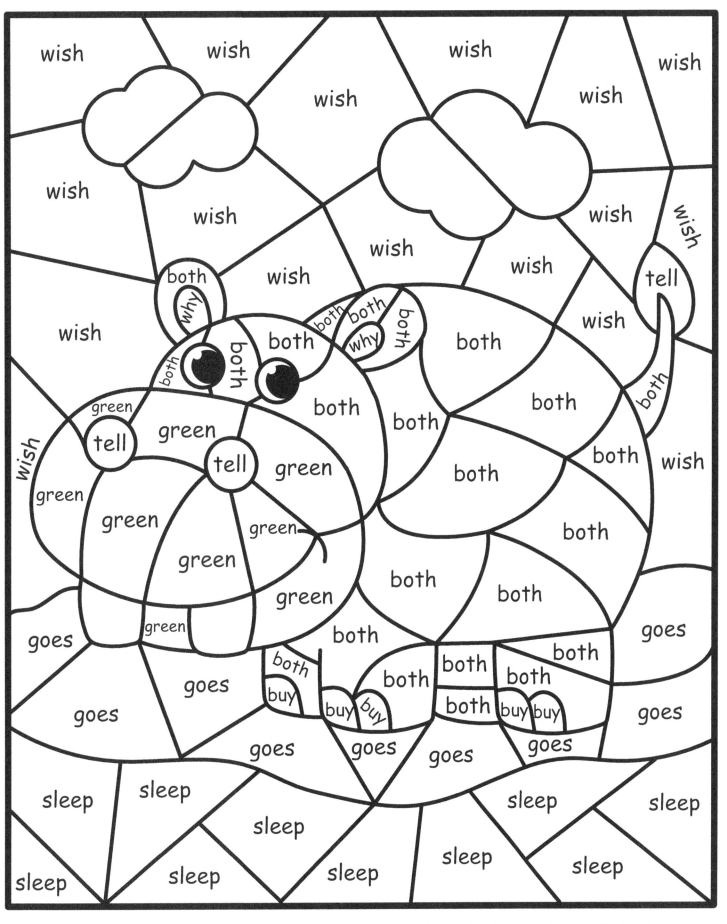

both - dark purple   sleep - dark brown   tell - black   buy - light brown

goes - dark green   green - light purple   why - pink   wish - light blue

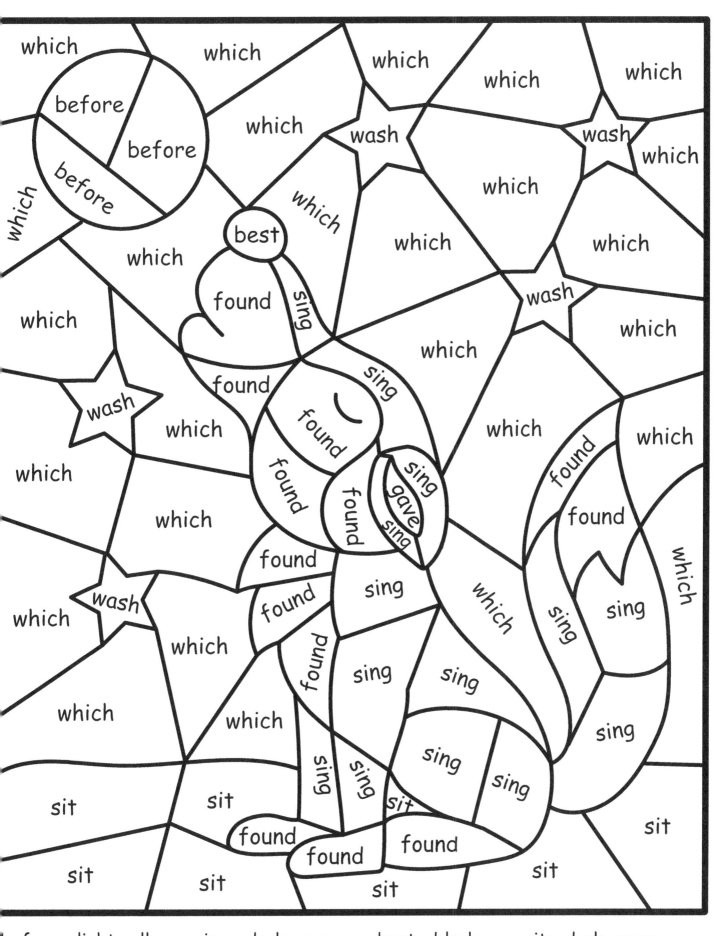

before - light yellow   sing - dark gray   best - black   sit - dark green

found - light gray   wash - dark yellow   gave - pink   which - dark blue

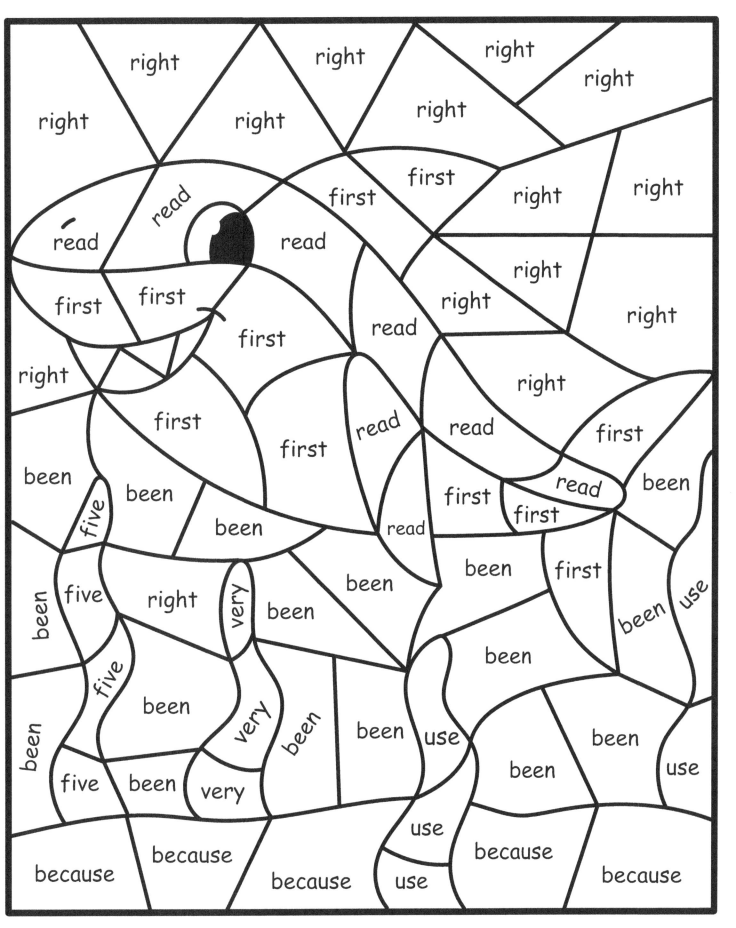

because - orange   read - dark gray   been - dark blue   right - light blue

first - light gray   use - yellow   five- dark green   very - light green

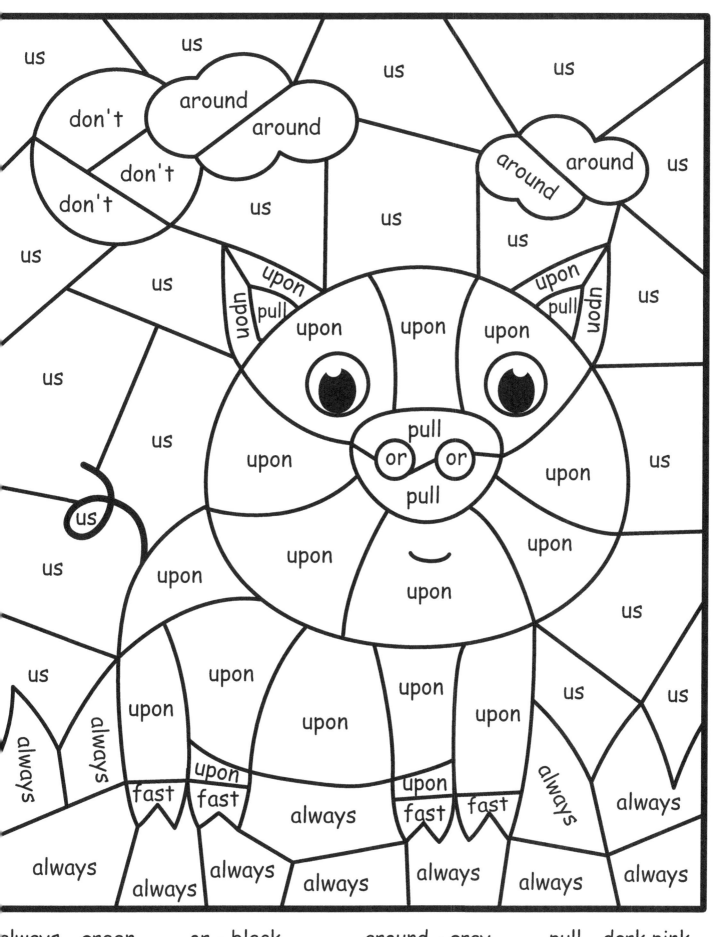

always - green   or - black   around - gray   pull - dark pink

don't - yellow   upon - light pink   fast - brown   us - blue

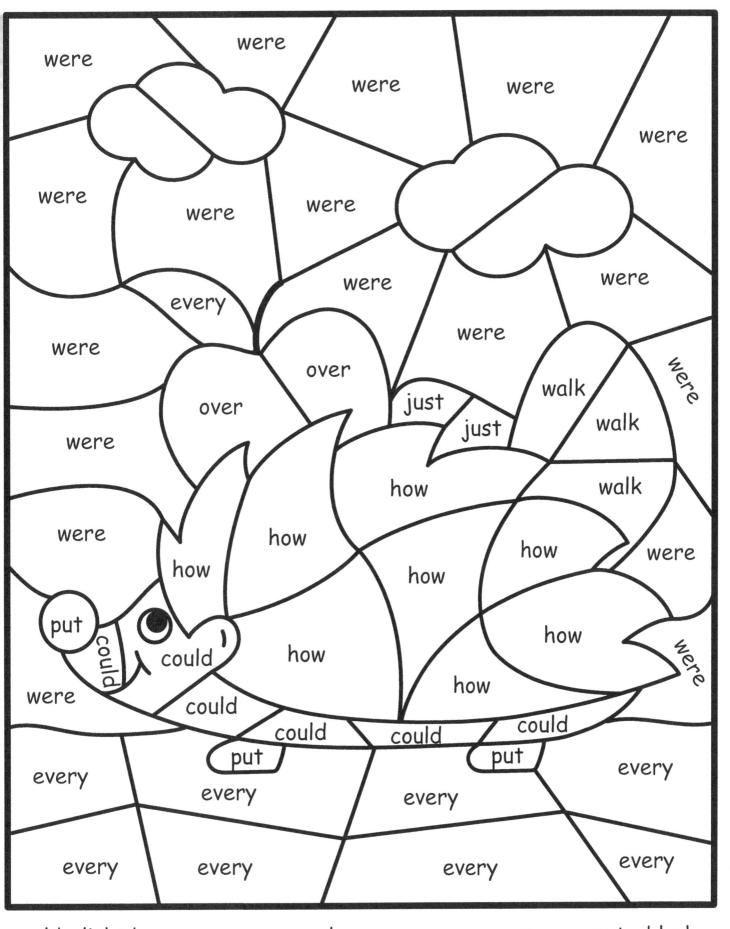

could - light brown   over - red   every - green   put - black

how - dark brown   walk - orange   just - yellow   were - blue

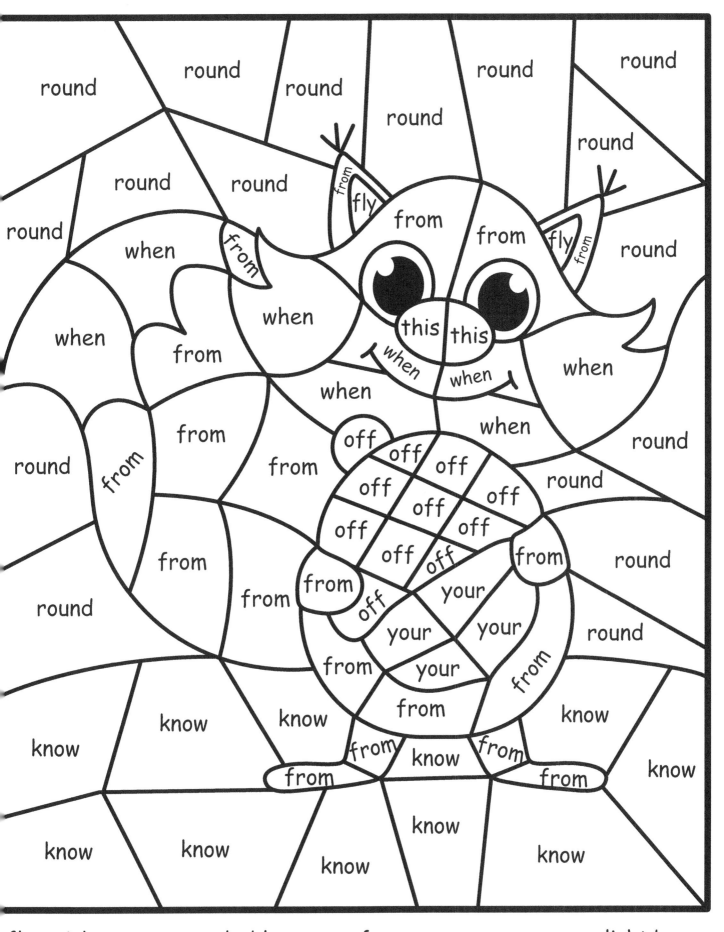

fly - pink   round - blue   from - orange   your - light brown

know - green   when - yellow   off - dark brown   this - black

Made in the USA
Monee, IL
01 August 2023

40323577R00059